SIMPLE STEPS

TOWARD A HEALTHIER EARTH

MORE THAN 55 PLANET-PROTECTING ACTIVITIES + 80 STICKERS

By
MOLLY SMITH

Illustrated by
TAD CARPENTER

Developed in collaboration with
the Natural Resources Defense Council

chronicle books · san francisco

Visit www.simplesteps.org to find more ways that you and your family can help protect the planet.

Copyright © 2010 by Chronicle Books LLC.
All rights reserved. No part of this book may be reproduced in any form without written permission from the publisher.

Book design by **ELOISE LEIGH**.
Typeset in Flama.
Text by **MOLLY SMITH**.
Illustrations by **TAD CARPENTER**.
The illustrations in this book were rendered in ink.
ISBN 978-0-8118-7141-9

Manufactured by Toppan Leefung, Da Ling Shan Town, China, in December 2009.

10 9 8 7 6 5 4 3 2 1

This product conforms to CPSIA 2008.

Chronicle Books LLC
680 Second Street, San Francisco, California 94107

www.chroniclekids.com

contents

INTRODUCTION
4

ENERGY AND CLIMATE
6

WATER AND OCEANS
22

LAND AND ANIMALS
36

HEALTH AND FOOD
50

WASTE AND RECYCLING
62

ANSWERS
76

INTRODUCTION

Global warming, greenhouse gases, climate change—you've probably been hearing a lot of talk about the environment. Some of it sounds kind of scary. You may feel like you're just one person in a big world. How can you possibly make a difference?

One person makes all sorts of little choices every day that can help or harm the planet we live on. We just have to learn what helps and what harms, and change our choices accordingly. That's one good reason to be optimistic about the future. As we pay more attention to the environment, we realize that there is so much each one of us can do to help it!

Inside this book, you'll find lots of information about all the things that can help and hurt the environment. By doing the activities, you'll find out what's going on with the earth, the air, and the water—and how you fit in.

Some of the activities use the stickers you'll find in the middle of this book. The stickers are labeled with the page number they're supposed to be used on.

At the end of each chapter, you'll discover a list of **SIMPLE STEPS**. These are tips to help you live a greener life. Small changes in your everyday life can become regular habits. Before you know it, you're making a difference in the big picture without even thinking about it!

HI, I'M BUZZLE BEE!

LOOK FOR ME THROUGHOUT THIS BOOK.

JUST LIKE SOME BEES GATHER POLLEN, I GATHER INFORMATION. SOMETIMES I WILL GIVE YOU HINTS TO HELP YOU COMPLETE AN ACTIVITY. SOMETIMES I WILL GIVE YOU FUN FACTS OR BACKGROUND BUZZ. REMEMBER THAT EVERYTHING YOU LEARN WILL HELP YOU TO BE MORE AWARE OF THE ENVIRONMENT. THIS WILL HELP YOU MAKE GREAT DECISIONS ABOUT HOW TO MAKE EARTH A BETTER PLACE.

YOU CAN **BEE** THE CHANGE!

ENERGY AND CLIMATE

WHAT IS ENERGY?

Energy moves cars. It lights a room. It keeps popsicles frozen in our freezers. It plays music and movies. Scientists define *energy* as "the ability to do work." People have learned how to change energy from one form to another so that we can do work more easily. So, for example, natural gas can be turned into electricity to power your home!

WHAT IS CLIMATE?

Climate tells us what the weather is usually like in a place at certain times of the year. For example, we know that Burlington, Vermont, is usually cold and snowy during the winter. Climate is affected by many factors, including latitude, elevation, and nearby bodies of water. What is the climate like where you live?

WHAT DOES ENERGY HAVE TO DO WITH CLIMATE?

Many forms of energy resources are harmful to the environment. One group of energy resources is called "fossil fuels." Natural gas, coal, and oil are fossil fuels because they were formed from the remains of ancient plants and animals. Burning fossil fuels releases carbon dioxide into the air. Too much carbon dioxide is one of the main causes of global warming.

Over the past 100 years, the average temperature on Earth has gone up slightly. Many scientists think this trend could continue if we do not work to help slow it down. A warmer Earth may lead to changes in precipitation patterns (like too much or too little rain). It could also lead to a rise in sea level and have a wide-ranging impact on wildlife and wildlands.

Whenever we save energy, we cut down on the demand for gas, oil, and coal. Burning less of these fossil fuels means less carbon dioxide gets released into the air.

THIS IS HOW WE USE IT

What sources of energy do we use to keep our homes and cars running? Below you'll find four examples. **UNSCRAMBLE THE NAME OF EACH ENERGY SOURCE.**

 SGALEONI
gasoline

 ILO
oil

 LETERTCIICY
Electricity

 PNPOERA
Propane

CHOOSE A COLOR FOR EACH WAY WE USE ENERGY AT HOME AND FILL IN THE KEY BELOW

The pie chart below is divided to show how energy is used in homes. Can you figure out which type of home energy usage matches each percentage? **USE COLOR CODES TO COLOR IN THE PIE CHART.**

- WATER HEATER
- LIGHTING AND APPLIANCES
- REFRIGERATION
- AIR CONDITIONING
- HEATING

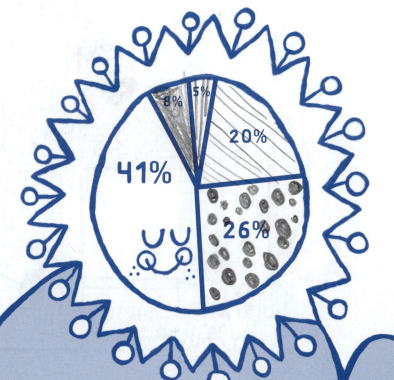

HINTS:
- *The two smallest sections have to do with cooling.*
- *Heating uses a little more than twice the energy used by the water heater.*

WHAT A WASTE!

Saving energy begins at home. Look at this house. Which room in the house do you think typically uses the most energy?
DRAW AN ARROW POINTING TO IT.

Imagine that no one is home. Can you find places where energy is being wasted?
CIRCLE THEM.

Do you see places where heat or cooled air could escape?
MAKE A BOX AROUND THEM.

Do you see an energy vampire (described below) in this house?
PLACE AN "ENERGY VAMPIRE" STICKER ON IT.

Do you know what an energy vampire is? If you leave any kind of chargers plugged in, you do. Always unplug a charger when you are not using it. It is still sucking a trickle of energy out of your home even if nothing is attached to it! Hunt for energy vampires lurking in your home. Place an ENERGY VAMPIRE STICKER on them to remind yourself to unplug them.

EVERYDAY ENERGY

Which home appliances do you think use the most energy? The least? See if you can put the appliances below in order from biggest energy sucker to smallest. **START WITH "1" FOR THE BIGGEST ENERGY SUCKER AND FINISH WITH "5" FOR THE SMALLEST.**

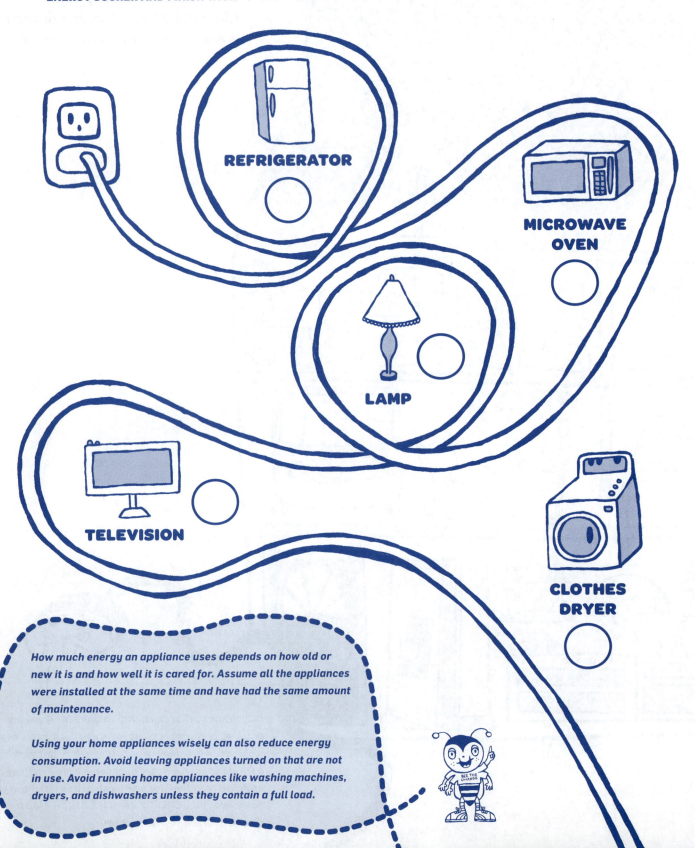

How much energy an appliance uses depends on how old or new it is and how well it is cared for. Assume all the appliances were installed at the same time and have had the same amount of maintenance.

Using your home appliances wisely can also reduce energy consumption. Avoid leaving appliances turned on that are not in use. Avoid running home appliances like washing machines, dryers, and dishwashers unless they contain a full load.

ENERGY IN MOTION

Much of the world's energy is used to power transportation. For example, more than 20 percent of the energy used in the United States goes to moving people and goods from one place to another. Which types of transportation need fuel to work? **CIRCLE THEM. THEN DRAW A STAR ON THE BIGGEST ENERGY USER.**

DREAM CAR

Engineers have been working hard to develop new ways to think about fueling transportation. Imagine you're a car engineer who has been asked to create a "dream car" that uses energy efficiently. Think about how it could be fueled and what special features it might have. **DRAW YOUR DREAM CAR BELOW AND LABEL ALL THE FEATURES THAT ARE GOOD FOR THE ENVIRONMENT.**

DREAM HOUSE

Imagine you're an architect who has been asked to design an energy-efficient, environmentally friendly house. **DRAW YOUR DREAM HOUSE BELOW AND LABEL ALL THE FEATURES THAT ARE GOOD FOR THE ENVIRONMENT. THINK ABOUT THE YARD, TOO!**

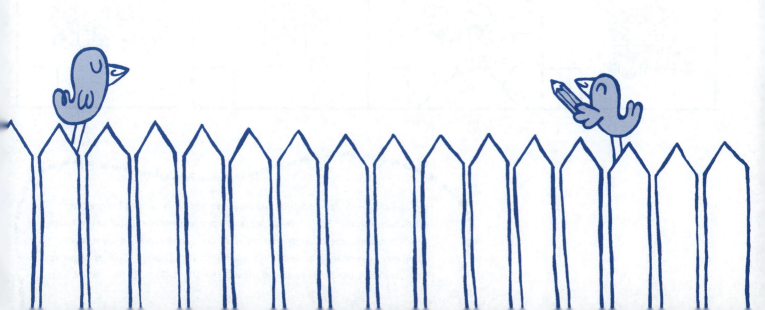

RESOURCE RUNDOWN

There are two basic kinds of energy resources available on Earth:

RENEWABLE energy resources will not run out. However, large amounts of them are needed to produce small amounts of energy. Wood is an example of a renewable resource. Just remember that "renewable" does not mean we can use the resource carelessly. When we cut down trees faster than they are growing, we harm the environment.

NON-RENEWABLE energy resources cannot be replaced once they are used up. There are only so much of them in the world. For example, coal is a non-renewable energy resource, since it takes millions of years to create.

WRITE "R" FOR RENEWABLE OR "NR" FOR NON-RENEWABLE BELOW EACH PICTURE TO DESCRIBE WHAT KIND OF ENERGY EACH PICTURE REPRESENTS.

Fossil fuels were formed 300 million years ago. That's long before the dinosaurs roamed Earth! Fossil fuels are made up of plant and animal matter. When prehistoric plants and animals died, their bodies decomposed. They were eventually buried under many layers of earth. Millions of years later, we have the three forms of fossil fuel: OIL, NATURAL GAS, and COAL.

ENERGY PUZZLER

SOLVE EACH CLUE AND FILL IN THE PUZZLE WITH THE CORRECT ENERGY WORD. SOME OF THESE ARE TRICKY! LOOK AT THE LIST BELOW TO HELP GUIDE YOU.

METHANE URANIUM OIL COAL BIOMASS ETHANOL ELECTRICITY HYDROPOWER fossil fuels

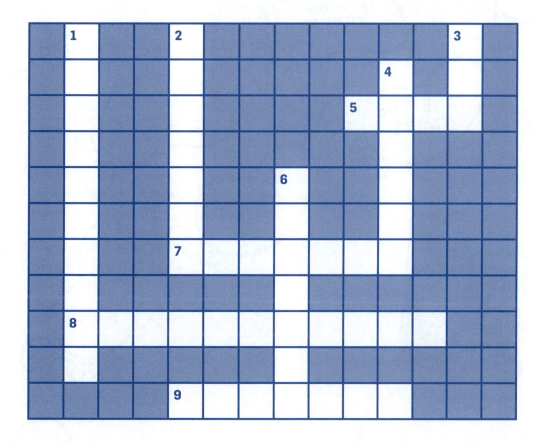

DOWN
1. Energy that comes from moving water
2. A gas that can come from animal waste
3. A black, liquid fossil fuel found deep in the earth
4. Coal, oil, and natural gas are _____ fuels
6. A heavy, naturally radioactive element

ACROSS
5. Fossil fuel formed by the breakdown of plant matter
7. A gasoline alternative; can be made from sugarcane, corn, or barley
8. Energy resulting from the movement of electrons through matter
9. Plant or animal material that can be used as a renewable resource

CARBON FOOTPRINTS

Have you heard of a carbon footprint? Your carbon footprint is all the greenhouse gas emissions caused directly by what you do and how you use energy every day! You can reduce the size of your footprint by using less energy and also by changing the way you use energy. **LOOK AT THESE FOOTPRINTS. COLOR THE POSITIVE STEPS IN GREEN.**

GREENHOUSE EFFECT

Have you ever been in a greenhouse? It uses the sun to stay hot even when the weather outside is cold. It does this by trapping the sun's energy. Look at the diagram below. It explains the greenhouse effect on Earth.

COLOR THE ARROW THAT SHOWS...

DIRECT HEAT FROM THE SUN IN **YELLOW**

HOT AIR TRAPPED IN ATMOSPHERE IN **RED**

HEAT ESCAPING FROM EARTH IN **GREEN**

The atmosphere is the air that covers Earth somewhat like a blanket. It is a thin layer of mixed gases. These gases make up the air we breathe. This thin layer also helps Earth from becoming too hot or too cold. "Greenhouse gases" make Earth warmer by trapping energy in the atmosphere. When there's too much of these gases, Earth can start getting warmer than we want it to be!

NATURAL DISASTER JUMBLE

Scientists carefully study weather patterns to help predict the future of our changing climate. Some natural disasters may be growing in intensity as a result of global warming.

WRITE THE ANSWER TO EACH CLUE ON THE BLANK LINES. THEN UNSCRAMBLE THE CIRCLED LETTERS TO ANSWER THE QUESTION AT THE BOTTOM.

I am the study of the atmosphere and all its phenomena, including weather and how to forecast it.

TEERMOYOOLG _ _ _ _ _ _ _ _ _ _

I am a period without rainfall in a certain area. I can create shortages in water supplies, destroy crops, and cause hunger.

UDORHTG _ _ _ _ _ _ _

I am a violent rotating column of air.

ROODTAN _ _ _ _ _ _ _

I am any kind of water that falls from clouds.

INPTPERCIOTAI _ _ _ _ _ _ _ _ _ _ _ _ _

I am an overflow of water resulting from days of heavy rain, melting snows, and/or rising bodies of water. Global warming may result in more of me in the future.

LOFOD _ _ _ _ _

I am a storm with heavy rain and swirling winds. Scientists believe storms like me have been increasing in intensity in the past several decades.

REUHNRICA _ _ _ _ _ _ _ _ _

I am an unusual warming of Pacific waters, and I have a Spanish name. I have been credited for one of the hottest years on record, 1998.

EÑOL NI _ _ _ _ _ _

WHAT IS A HURRICANE IN THE WESTERN PACIFIC OCEAN CALLED?

_ _ _ _ _ _ _

THINK GLOBALLY

The United States is the largest source of pollution contributing to global warming. The population of the United States is just 4 percent of the world's population, yet each year it produces more than 20 percent of the carbon dioxide pollution from burning fossil fuels such as petroleum, coal, or natural gas.

How do you think other countries stack up? Look at this list of 20 countries. Which do you think are the 10 countries with the worst annual air pollution emissions? **COLOR THEM IN RED.**

SIMPLE STEPS

CHANGE A LIGHTBULB

A compact florescent lightbulb, or CFL, uses 75 percent less energy than a traditional bulb to produce the same amount of light. If every home in the United States replaced just one lightbulb with a CFL, it would save enough energy to light more than 3 million homes for an entire year. This could prevent greenhouse gas emissions equal to that of more than 800,000 cars. See if you can replace at least 5 lightbulbs in your house with CFLs, if you're not using them already.

GET MOVING

Walking, bicycling, or riding a skateboard or anything else that is "people powered" instead of choosing a motor-powered vehicle reduces the amount of carbon dioxide released into the atmosphere. Plus, it's good exercise. Try walking or taking public transportation instead of using the car the next time you're going out with friends.

UNPLUG AND SHUT IT OFF

Keep electronics chargers unplugged until you need them. Turn off lights, computers, and TVs when they aren't being used. Use power strips to switch off office equipment, home theater equipment, and stereos when you're not using them. If all of these appliances are running all the time, they use about the same amount of electricity as one 75- or 100-watt lightbulb running continuously.

GET GROWING

Planting trees is fun and a great way to reduce greenhouse gases, since trees absorb carbon dioxide from the air. Trees can shade your home to reduce the need for air conditioning. Why not plant a new tree in your backyard or get permission to plant one in front of your school?

GIVE YOUR SCHOOL A REPORT CARD!

Use the following checklist to evaluate your school's impact on the climate. Ask your teacher or some classmates to help you answer some of the questions. Then start a project to write a letter to your principal or school officials with suggestions for how to improve your school's impact on the climate.

	USES CFL BULBS
	USES ENERGY-EFFICIENT APPLIANCES
	ALLOWS BUSES TO IDLE IN FRONT OF SCHOOL
	USES RENEWABLE RESOURCES FOR HEATING
	PROVIDES CLASSES ABOUT THE ENVIRONMENT
	ENCOURAGES CARPOOLING
	TURNS OFF LIGHTS IN ROOMS NOT BEING USED

Water and Oceans

It is hard to think of anything more important to life on Earth than freshwater! All living things need water to survive. More than 70 percent of Earth's surface is covered in water. More than 50 percent of the human body is water. The average person cannot survive much longer than three days without fresh water.

FRESHWATER

Even though much of Earth is covered by water, nearly 97 percent of that is nondrinkable salt water found in the oceans. Another 2 percent is frozen in ice caps and glaciers. That leaves just 1 percent for all living things to drink and use.

As with many other natural renewable resources, we are putting great demands on our freshwater supplies. Two reasons for this are population growth and pollution of the freshwater we do have. Can you think of other reasons? We must learn to use water more efficiently and to keep it clean and usable. Otherwise, we could use up all the freshwater we have before it has time to renew itself!

OCEANS

Earth's oceans are home to more than a million known species of plants and animals. Because much of the ocean is still unexplored, scientists believe there may be as many as millions more undiscovered species! Protecting the oceans and the plant and animal life that depend on them is important. Less than 1 percent of the ocean is protected from fishing and pollution. Fish and marine mammals like whales and dolphins need places that are safe to live and reproduce.

WATER WORKS

23

Earth has a limited amount of water. That water keeps going around and around from the land to the sky and back. This process is called the water cycle.

READ THE DEFINITIONS FOR EACH PART OF THE WATER CYCLE. THEN FILL IN THE LABELS ON THE WATER CYCLE DIAGRAM BELOW.

TRANSPIRATION	is how plants lose water out of their leaves into the atmosphere.
CONDENSATION	is when water vapor in the air turns into liquid. **HINT:** *This goes on two different lines in the diagram.*
EVAPORATION	is when the sun heats up a body of water and turns it into vapor.
PRECIPITATION	happens when so much water has condensed that the air cannot hold it anymore and releases hail, mist, rain, sleet, or snow.
ACCUMULATION	is when water pools in large bodies of water.
SURFACE RUNOFF	is when rain, melted snow, or other water flows into surface streams, rivers, or canals.

DRIP DETECTIVES

There are many places in the world where people do not have clean, fresh water at the turn of a faucet. In other places, water goes down the drain without a thought. For example, the average person living in Canada uses more than six times as much water a day than the average person in India and more than 30 times as much as a rural villager in Kenya. People in the United States consume the most water, with an average of 100 gallons a day! How much of the water you use is really necessary? Complete these activities to find out how much water you could save each day. Become a drip detective!

DON'T BRUSH THIS OFF

How much water can you save by turning off the faucet while brushing your teeth?

PLACE A LARGE CONTAINER IN YOUR SINK UNDER THE FAUCET. TURN ON THE FAUCET WHILE YOU BRUSH YOUR TEETH AND KEEP IT RUNNING UNTIL YOU ARE FINISHED. USE A MEASURING CUP TO MEASURE THE AMOUNT OF WATER IN THE CONTAINER.

How much water could be saved each time you brush your teeth? _____ CUPS

Multiply that number by 2: _____ CUPS EACH DAY

Multiply that number by 7: _____ CUPS EACH WEEK

How many gallons of water could be saved in one year? _____ GALLONS

HINT: *16 cups = 1 gallon*

An open faucet lets about 5 gallons of water flow every 2 minutes! Do you think a drippy faucet can't waste that much water? Think again. A faucet that drips once per second can waste 8 gallons of water a day!

How many gallons could it waste each year? You do the math.

TWO TOILET TRICKS

Be sure to get an adult's permission before trying these activities!

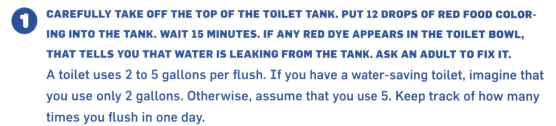

1 **CAREFULLY TAKE OFF THE TOP OF THE TOILET TANK. PUT 12 DROPS OF RED FOOD COLORING INTO THE TANK. WAIT 15 MINUTES. IF ANY RED DYE APPEARS IN THE TOILET BOWL, THAT TELLS YOU THAT WATER IS LEAKING FROM THE TANK. ASK AN ADULT TO FIX IT.**

A toilet uses 2 to 5 gallons per flush. If you have a water-saving toilet, imagine that you use only 2 gallons. Otherwise, assume that you use 5. Keep track of how many times you flush in one day.

How much water did you use? _____ GALLONS

2 **NOW, FILL UP A 1-GALLON WATER JUG AND PLACE IT IN THE TANK.**

This takes up room in the tank, preventing it from filling all the way. This saves 1 gallon each time you flush.

About how many gallons would this save you each day? _____ GALLONS

BATHERS BEWARE

Taking a bath can waste much more water than taking a shower. Try it out for yourself.

THE NEXT TIME YOU TAKE A BATH, MAKE A MARK AT THE WATER LINE. (BE SURE TO USE A BATHTUB CRAYON THAT WILL WASH AWAY EASILY!)

THE NEXT TIME YOU TAKE A SHOWER, KEEP THE DRAIN CLOSED AND MAKE A MARK WHERE THAT WATER LINE IS.

How do the bath and shower water lines compare? Time your next shower to be exactly five minutes. How does this water line compare? If everyone in the United States used just one less gallon of water per shower each day, that would save about 85 billion gallons of water per year!

How much do you think you personally could save? _____ GALLONS
HINT: Figure out how many days per week you shower and multiply that number by 52.

DOWN THE DRAIN

The things we send down the drain, whether through the kitchen sink or a storm drain, do not disappear. Everything that travels into the local water supply can stay in that very water, which is meant for drinking. Look at each scene. Which products are okay to send down the drain? Which might poison the water? **COLOR THE PATHS OF EARTH-FRIENDLY PRODUCTS GREEN, AND THOSE OF POISON PRODUCTS RED.**

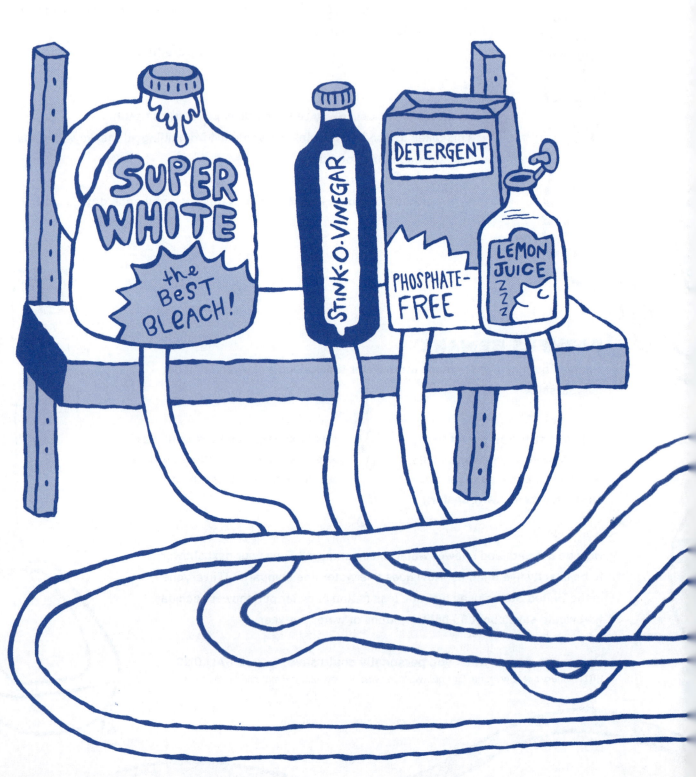

HINT: *Phosphates are found in cleaning products and fertilizers, among other things. When they end up in lakes or rivers, they can cause an overgrowth of algae. This can use up a lot of the oxygen in the water—and aquatic animals need that oxygen to live.*

GO FISH!

Many fish that were once plentiful in number have had major population declines in recent decades. Much of this is due to overfishing, destruction of habitats, and harmful fishing practices, such as trawling. Trawling is a way of fishing with large nets. Trawling is often used to catch shrimp or herring.

When fishermen are fishing for one species, they often catch other creatures that live nearby. These could be other fish species or other marine creatures, such as dolphins, who are looking for their own fish dinner. If these other sea creatures become entangled in the nets or get caught on fishhooks, they could drown. This is called "bycatch," and it is a global problem.

The fish shapes below contain letters that spell out the names of eight kinds of fish. Four are not good to catch and eat because their populations are threatened by overfishing. Four are better choices to catch and eat because their populations are carefully managed, or, in other words, they're "sustainable."

29

PUT TOGETHER THE LETTERS IN THESE FISH (IN ORDER FROM LEFT TO RIGHT ACROSS EACH ROW, FROM TOP TO BOTTOM) TO SPELL FOUR FISH THAT HAVE THREATENED POPULATIONS.

_____

_____

_____

_____

PUT TOGETHER THE LETTERS IN THESE FISH (FROM LEFT TO RIGHT ACROSS EACH ROW, FROM TOP TO BOTTOM) TO SPELL FOUR FISH THAT ARE SUSTAINABLE.

_____

_____

_____

_____

DON'T CATCH ANY DOLPHINS! THEY'RE "BYCATCH," SO THEIR LETTERS ARE NOT NEEDED.

THE PROBLEM WITH PLASTIC

Billions of plastic bags alone end up in the ocean each year. Plastic does not break down easily or entirely. In fact, every bit of plastic that has ever been made is still with us in some way! Some countries, such as China, and large cities, such as San Francisco, have banned plastic grocery bags for this very reason. Think about how many plastic bags your family uses. **KEEP TRACK OF HOW MANY COME INTO YOUR HOME EACH WEEK.**

Plastic bags from the grocery store: _____ BAGS

Other plastic bags: _____ BAGS

Total: _____ BAGS

Now multiply that number by 52 to find out about how many plastic bags your family uses each year: _____ BAGS

MUCH OF THE TRASH FLOATING IN EARTH'S OCEANS IS PLASTIC. FIND AND CIRCLE EACH PIECE OF PLASTIC IN THIS OCEAN SCENE.

Large plastic bags can be mistaken for jellyfish by animals, such as sea turtles, who eat them. Other kinds of plastic, such as caps, get stuck in the throats of sea animals and birds. To help with this problem, you can make sure all plastic you use is properly recycled. Some grocery stores have special collection bins for plastic bags.

THAR SHE BLOWS!

Whales are beautiful, mysterious creatures of the deep sea. Unfortunately, many species were hunted nearly to the point of extinction. Hunting whales is now illegal, but many whales are still suffering because of the destruction of their habitat. Read the description for each of the different endangered whales. **PLACE THE MATCHING WHALE STICKER ABOVE THE DESCRIPTION AND WRITE ITS NAME ON THE LINE.**

This whale is unusual in its appearance because it does not have a single, large dorsal fin.

This whale is the largest creature to have ever lived on Earth. That includes the dinosaurs!

This whale is named for the shape of its body. It's also famous for its beautiful and complex songs.

This Arctic whale is best known for its long spiral tusk.

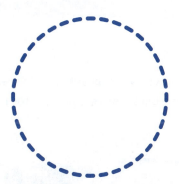

This Arctic whale uses its huge head to break ice in order to breathe.

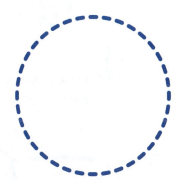

This whale got its unfortunate name for being considered the correct whale to hunt.

Whales and other marine mammals rely greatly on their hearing for survival. Sound is how they find food and their way about the ocean. Manmade sound waves can drown out the noises that marine mammals rely on for their survival. This can cause serious injury and even death. These harmful sounds can come from air guns that are used in oil exploration or naval submarines and ships emitting sonar noise.

MELTING MADNESS

Due to the greenhouse effect, average temperatures in the Arctic region, around Earth's North Pole, are rising twice as fast as they are anywhere else in the world. Locate the Arctic region on a globe or a map. Where is it relative to where you live? Then look at this picture that shows the size of the summer ice cap in the Arctic Sea in 1979 (the shape is not exact). Since that time, it has shrunk 20 percent. **USE THIS FACT TO COLOR THE PORTION OF THE ICE CAP THAT YOU THINK REMAINS.**

TRY THIS EXPERIMENT. PLACE TWO ICE CUBES IN THE SUNLIGHT TO MELT. PUT ONE ON A SHEET OF WHITE PAPER. PUT THE OTHER ON A SHEET OF BLACK PAPER. RECORD THE TIME IT TAKES EACH ICE CUBE TO MELT.

Which one melted more rapidly? Why do you think that happened? How can this experiment help you understand some of the effects of the melting ice cap?

The melting of the Arctic ice cap is speeding up global warming. Snow and ice usually form a protective, cooling layer that reflects the sun's rays back into space (like the white paper in the experiment above.) Without snow and ice, Earth's surface absorbs more sunlight and gets hotter.

OCEAN FOOD WEB

All living things on land, air, and in water are connected through a great food web. Life depends on the transfer of energy from one living creature to another. This transfer of energy takes place whenever an animal living in the wild eats another animal or a plant. Larger predators eat smaller animals, and smaller animals live on plants or even smaller prey. The biggest to the smallest microscopic creatures are all part of the food web.

IMAGINE LIVING ON ANTARCTICA, THE COLDEST, WINDIEST CONTINENT. LOOK AT THE ANTARCTICA FOOD WEB. PLACE A PLANT OR ANIMAL STICKER WHERE YOU THINK IT BELONGS IN EACH PART OF THE WEB.

Many people enjoy or depend on eating seafood. However, careless overfishing has destroyed much of the ocean's resources. Ninety percent of the world's stock of larger fish, such as tuna, has disappeared from the oceans. Fish fans can help solve this problem by eating smaller fish, such as sardines, that are lower on the food chain.

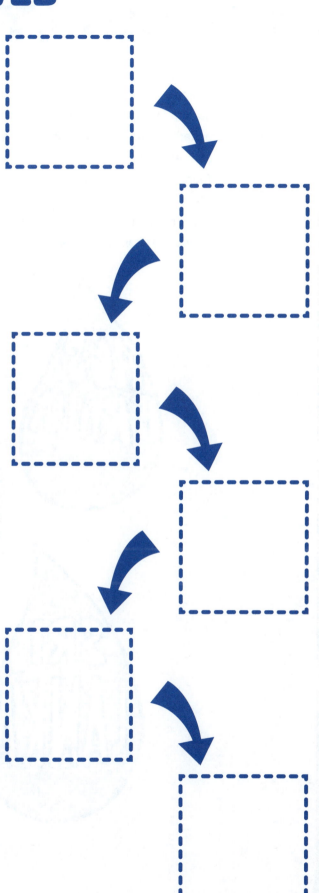

THINK GLOBALLY

Over a billion people on Earth do not have access to fresh, clean water. That is about 20 percent of the world's population. This problem does not just affect one part of the world. Roughly one-third of people live in "water stressed" countries. The shortage is greatest in developing countries, especially in Sub-Saharan Africa and South Asia. For most people in North America and Europe, getting clean water is as easy as turning on a faucet. However, in many places around the globe, particularly rural areas, people walk miles each day just to get it. This may not make sense when you look at a globe. After all, it's mostly blue! In two of the countries listed below, the majority of the citizens did not have access to clean drinking water in 2004. **CAN YOU COLOR THE NAMES OF THE TWO COUNTRIES?**

SIMPLE STEPS

LOAD IT UP

Dishwashers and washing machines are two of our biggest water-guzzlers. It is important to always run full loads. Don't waste water and energy on a pair of jeans or a couple dirty dishes. It is also a mistake to waste water by prewashing or rinsing dishes before putting them in the dishwasher. If you must rinse thoroughly, do so in a pan or closed sink. Don't let the water run.

CLOSE THAT HOSE

There are many ways we can save water outdoors. Make sure outdoor faucets aren't dripping. Use buckets when washing cars. This uses much less water than letting the hose run. Don't overwater your lawn. Use mulch to keep water in around plants. And never water the lawn when the weather is doing it for you! Also, use a broom or a brush to clean off pavement. Save water for the living things that need it!

CHECK YOUR HOME

Is your household water- and ocean-friendly? Use the checklist to help you find out and then decide how you can help turn bad habits into good habits.

Do you or does anyone in your household . . .

	YES	NO	SOME-TIMES
RUN LESS THAN FULL WASHING MACHINES?			
RUN WATER WHILE BRUSHING TEETH OR SHAVING?			
WATER THE LAWN ON COOL, RAINY, OR WINDY DAYS OR AT NOON?			
RUN THE HOSE WHILE WASHING THE CAR?			
TAKE LONG SHOWERS OR FULL BATHS?			
RINSE FOOD FROM DISHES WITH THE WATER RUNNING?			
DUMP HARSH CHEMICALS (LIKE PAINT OR MOTOR OIL) DOWN THE DRAIN?			
EAT LARGE AMOUNTS OF "BIG" FISH LIKE TUNA?			
THROW PLASTIC IN WITH THE REGULAR GARBAGE?			

LAND AND ANIMALS

LAND

As the human population grows, we are making more and more demands on the land. Modern progress is threatening to destroy places that support life and help regulate the climate. We are creating huge global changes, such as cutting down massive amounts of forested lands and destroying habitats. Habitats can be big or small—can you find one or more in your own backyard or school yard?

Tropical rain forests are important habitats on Earth. The rain forests are shrinking every day, which impacts all of Earth's atmosphere. Take a few deep breaths. Rain forests act like lungs in reverse. They take in large amounts of carbon dioxide, a poisonous gas that mammals (including you) exhale, and change it into clean, breathable air through photosynthesis. In order to keep our climate healthy, we must work to protect all parts of Earth.

ANIMALS

Do you love animals? Some animals die out naturally because newer species are better at competing for living space and food. Remember the food web? Others become extinct because of changes in the planet or because of natural disasters.

Today, the major threats that animals face are largely caused by humans. These threats include hunting, pollution, and encroachment on natural habitats. There are as many as 5,000 animal species facing extinction today. We must all work together to keep them and the land where they live safe.

ENDANGERED ANIMALS

Endangered animals are at risk of becoming extinct. These animals are put in different risk categories depending on how threatening their situation is. Read about some of the categories below. **USING THE CLUES TO GUIDE YOU, PLACE AN ANIMAL STICKER IN EACH SPACE.**

EXTINCT   The *last remaining member* of the species has died.

This was one of the largest bird species two centuries ago. It was known for its large flocks.

This sea mammal was last spotted in 1952.

ENDANGERED   The animal faces a *very high risk* of extinction in the near future.

These large mammals are known for walking on their knuckles.

This animal is rapidly losing its favorite food source: bamboo.

VULNERABLE   The animal faces a *high risk* of extinction.

These cats are the fastest land animals in the world.

This king of the African savanna has lost nearly half its population in the last 50 years.

POLLUTION POLICE

Pollution is anything that contaminates the land, water, or air and makes Earth, animals, and people less healthy. Some kinds of pollution, like smoke coming out of a smokestack, are obvious, while others may be harder to discover.

LOOK AT THIS SCENE. FIND AND CIRCLE ANYTHING YOU SEE THAT MIGHT BE POLLUTING THE ENVIRONMENT.

Noise pollution is a real environmental factor that you might not often think about. Noise disrupts animals in their natural habitats and can affect the way they live and search for food. It also causes stress—this is true for humans, too! Can you name five or more noise pollutants? What positive choices can you make to help reduce noise pollution in your home, neighborhood, and school?

TAKE ME HOME

Earth has many unique kinds of habitats. Each habitat is home to marvelous animals that have adapted to that specific environment. If these areas are not protected, the animals may not be able to adapt and may become extinct. **PLACE THE ANIMAL STICKERS IN THE CORRECT HABITAT. THERE ARE TWO ANIMALS FOR EACH AREA.**

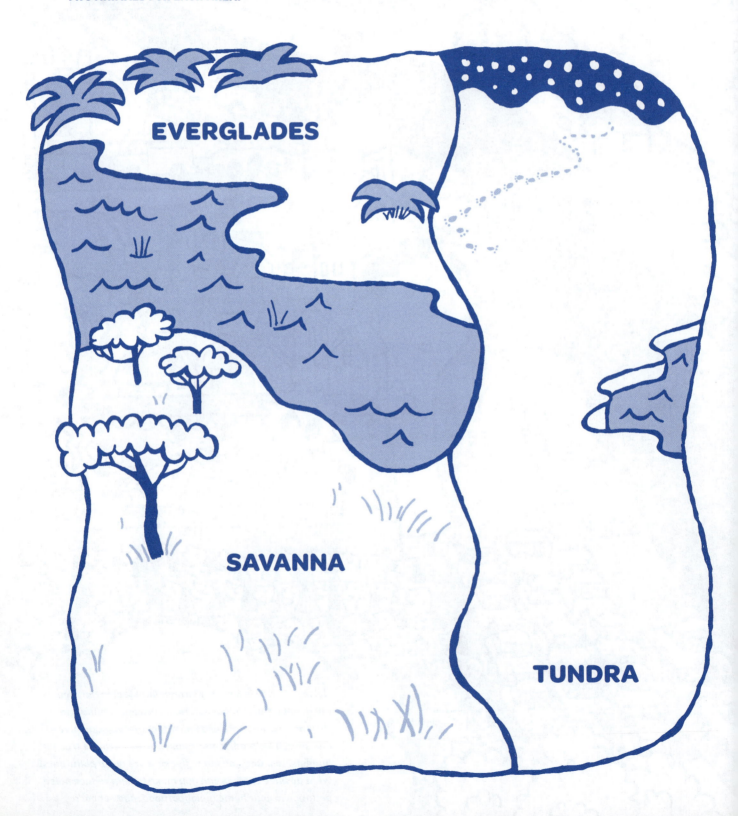

THE BUZZ ON BEES

Have you ever tried to enjoy a summer picnic or an outdoor snack only to be harassed by the buzz of pesky bees? You swat, you run, but they just won't leave you alone. Maybe you've wished there was no such thing as bees.

It might surprise you to find out that some bees actually are becoming rare and endangered! While this may seem like good news for picnics, it's not. Bees are responsible for pollinating the plants on farms that grow our food and are considered a crucial part of the food chain. In fact, experts say that nearly one-third of everything we eat comes from plants pollinated by bees. **LOOK AT THE HIVE BELOW, AND FIND ALL OF THE THREATS BEES FACE IN THE MODERN WORLD.**

```
I H Q T W B U Z S M J M G G F
Y C D I S E A S E S F I N J R
D R R E T A M F T C U T N K Y
I F B W X M W L L C I E Y S M
M P W X B I S D W M H S I K D
J S E R I F T S E R O F P U T
K E U R B A N I Z A T I O N A
D E S M U L Q S Z V E T A K W
N R X I I H E W E Y K J U S I
S E D I C I T S E P T Q H P L
```

**PESTICIDES   SKUNKS   MITES
DISEASES   FOREST FIRES
URBANIZATION**

HINT: *Some are written backward.*

Without bees, some fruits and vegetables could disappear from the food supply! In 2004, there were not enough bees for the almond blossoms in California. You can help keep the bee population alive just by planting a few native plants or an herb garden in your own backyard or on a window box. Make sure to avoid using pesticides!

THE AMAZING RAIN FOREST

Earth's rain forests provide a home for more than 50 percent of the whole world's plants and animals! In fact, two and a half acres of land in a tropical rain forest could contain more species than a whole country in Europe. The rain forest has many different kinds of habitats within it. Scientists use the idea of four different zones to help us understand rain forests.

EMERGENTS

This zone includes the tops of the highest trees. It is a wonderful home for birds.

CANOPY

This zone includes the upper parts of the trees, which provide a leafy environment that is full of life. Many well-known animals, including mammals such as monkeys and small cats, are found in the canopy.

UNDERSTORY

This zone is a dark, cool environment under the largest leaves, but over the ground. It is perfect for amphibians. They can lay their eggs in water gathered in the leaves.

FOREST FLOOR

The thick leaves of the canopy make the ground layer of the rain forest a dark and humid place. This is where most of the largest animals live.

THE WONDERFUL WORLD OF WORMS

Do you think earthworms are gross? You might want to think again. Worms are an important part of the environment.

START

An earthworm moves by using its many (tiny!) legs.

Earthworms help water and air flow through soil.

Earthworms create nutrients that are necessary for fertile soil.

Earthworms have many teeth that they use to chew on plants.

Earthworms "breathe" through their skin.

Without the help of earthworms, plants and animals that die would not decompose.

TO SQUIRM YOUR WAY THROUGH THIS WORMY MAZE, ONLY GO DOWN PATHS WITH TRUE FACTS ABOUT EARTHWORMS, AND MAKE SURE TO PASS THROUGH ALL THE TRUE FACTS. WHEN YOU GET TO THE END, YOU MIGHT JUST DECIDE THAT EARTHWORMS ARE YOUR FRIENDS.

- Earthworms can destroy farm crops.
- Earthworms spread disease to people and animals.
- In one acre of land, there can be over a million earthworms.
- Earthworms can sometimes regrow a tail.
- Having earthworms in your garden is a bad sign.
- Earthworms swallow rocks to help break up their food.

FINISH
YEAH! YOU DID IT!

CRY WOLF

Think about some fairy tales or other stories you know about wolves. You might think of a wolf as the bad guy. Wolves have gotten a bad reputation. Do you think you know the truth about them?
LOOK AT THE STATEMENTS BELOW. WRITE "T" FOR TRUE OR "F" FOR FALSE NEXT TO EACH ONE.

 WOLVES KILL AS MANY AS 10 PEOPLE EACH YEAR.

 WOLVES ARE THE ANCESTORS OF ALL BREEDS OF DOMESTIC DOGS.

 WOLVES MAY SOON WIPE OUT ELK POPULATIONS.

 ALL GRAY WOLF POPULATIONS ARE STABLE AND DO NOT NEED PROTECTION.

 WOLVES ARE THE LARGEST MEMBERS OF THE CANINE FAMILY.

 WOLVES ONCE LIVED IN ALL OF WHAT IS CALLED THE LOWER 48 STATES IN THE UNITED STATES.

The wolves of the northern Rocky Mountains were taken off the U.S. endangered species list in Montana and Idaho in 2009. The Natural Resources Defense Council (NRDC) and other conservationists are going to court to fight this decision. Even though wolf populations have had some recovery, they feel that the number of wolves is far short of where it should be. Furthermore, the last time that the U.S. government took away the wolf's federal protection, in 2008, 110 wolves were hunted in 120 days.

THE GRIZZLY TRUTH

Experts estimate that as many as 100,000 grizzly bears lived in the United States (not including Alaska) during the 1800s. Today only about 1,500 grizzlies live in the 48 lower United States. There are about 60,000 grizzlies in the world.

Some grizzlies are killed by hunters even in places where they are protected by the government. This sometimes happens because the hunters are unable to tell them apart from black bears, which can be hunted legally at certain times. Can you tell the difference between a grizzly bear and a black bear? HINT: *A black bear has shorter, darker claws.*

WRITE THE NAME OF EACH BEAR ON THE LINE NEXT TO IT. THEN CIRCLE AT LEAST THREE OTHER DIFFERENCES BETWEEN THE TWO BEARS.

squatter
squarer snout
shaggier
brown bear

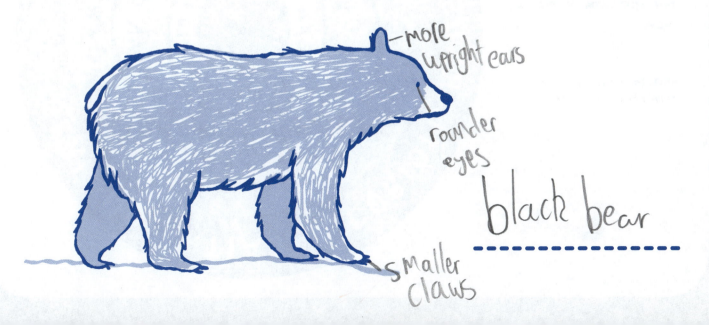

more upright ears
rounder eyes
black bear
smaller claws

THINK GLOBALLY

Rain forests can be found all over the world. It may surprise you that they can even be found as far north as Alaska and Canada. That is because not all rain forests are tropical. There are two major types of rain forest: temperate rain forests and tropical rain forests. The largest temperate rain forests are found on North America's Pacific Coast, but they exist in Asia, Africa, and other places.

Forests provide important products for human beings. Can you think of some? In fact, there are approximately 120 prescription drugs saving people's lives that come directly from rain forest plants. They also provide valuable services for the ecosystem. When a forest is intact, it is working for the planet— regulating the climate, stabilizing the soil, and cycling ecological nutrients, as well as providing a habitat for plant and animal species.

A major cause of global warming is logging and burning, called deforestation, around the world. Forests absorb carbon dioxide from the air. When they are cut down and burned, they release that carbon gas back into the atmosphere. Carbon absorbs infrared light and reflects it back to Earth, rather than releasing it out into space. This contributes to the warming of Earth's surface. It is estimated that one and a half acres of rain forest land is destroyed every second. It is also estimated that only about one-fifth of the world's original forest cover remains intact.

THE FIVE COUNTRIES WITH THE LARGEST SHARE OF THE WORLD'S DEFORESTATION ARE HIDDEN IN THE RINGS OF THIS TREE STUMP, ONE IN EACH RING. FIND THEM AND CIRCLE THEM.

HINT: *The names of the countries begin with B, Z, M, I, and N.*

SIMPLE STEPS

SHOP SMART
Forests are being destroyed to make toilet paper, facial tissues, paper towels, and other disposable paper products. You can help stop this destruction by encouraging your family to make smart shopping decisions. Always try to choose products made out of recycled materials!

DON'T LITTER
Respect Earth. Never, ever throw trash or garbage where it doesn't belong. Even the smallest bottle cap can kill an animal. Any amount of garbage threatens wildlands and wildlife.

GET INVOLVED
Join a local or national foundation that helps protect our lands and animals. You can easily find them on the Internet. Write to your local government officials, such as your town mayor or a senator, to tell them how you feel about protecting land and animals.

START A COMMUNITY CLEAN-UP
Helping the environment does not only mean protecting habitats or animals that are far away. Encourage your school or family and friends to sign up for tree-planting celebrations, or organize a group clean up of a local area that could use help, such as a beach, park, or empty lot. You can help the environment and have fun, too!

HEALTH AND FOOD

HEALTH

The air that we breathe, the water that we drink, and the land we live on all affect our health. Global warming is beginning to affect the health of the human race in a negative way. Insects that spread diseases and allergens that trigger asthma are thriving in a warmer world. By saving our environment, we are truly saving our well-being and ourselves.

FOOD

Now, more than ever, it is important to pay close attention to the food we decide to buy and eat. Modern technology has made it easier to transport and preserve food, but at what cost? Our demands for fast and easy foods may be poisoning our bodies with harsh chemicals.

You may know that what we eat has a huge impact on our health. But did you know our food choices also affect the health of the planet? By making smart food choices, we can both improve our individual health and curb global warming and pollution.

WHERE DID IT COME FROM?

51

When the fruits you like to eat are out of season locally, they may come from places very far away. Today, most of the food in your grocery store is labeled with its country of origin. Have you been paying attention? When you are at the grocery store, look for the labels that tell you where produce was grown. **TRY TO MATCH EACH OF THE FOODS LISTED HERE TO THE COUNTRY IT MOST LIKELY CAME FROM IF IT WAS OUT OF SEASON.**

ORANGES
This sweet treat often comes from the largest country in South America.

__ __ __ **B** __ __

CANTALOUPE
Mmmm, melon—all the way from Central America.

__ __ __ __ __ __ **M** __ __ __

GRAPES
You may think of grapes from the West Coast of California, but many grapes come from a West Coast country on a different continent.

__ **H** __ __ __

STRAWBERRIES
Many strawberries come from this neighbor of the United States.

__ __ __ __ **C** __

PEARS
Here's a tip. Pears often come from this country at the tip of South America.

__ __ __ __ __ __ __ **I** __ __

KIWI
This fruit is so popular on this island that its people sometimes call themselves "Kiwis"!

__ __ __ __ __ __ __ **D**

BANANA ADVENTURES

If you do not live in a tropical area, any banana you buy in a store most likely came from another country. Bananas are not grown commercially in many parts of the world. Costa Rica, Ecuador, and Honduras supply most of the world's banana imports.

LOOK AT THE MAP ON THE RIGHT TO SEE HOW FAR BUZZLE BEE'S BANANA TRAVELS.

1. The banana goes from the farm to the plant, then to the local port for shipment.

2. Then the banana spends at least a week on a refrigerated boat.

3. The banana arrives in a port and is held in a refrigeration facility there.

4. The banana travels from the port by refrigerated truck to Buzzle Bee's grocery store.

ABOUT HOW FAR DID BUZZLE BEE'S BANANA TRAVEL?

_____ MILES

Now see how far your bananas travel.

Where do you live? _____

Look at the labels on the bananas your family buys. Where did they come from? _____

About how far did the banana travel from its home country to your home? _____ MILES

HINT: *You can find food-miles calculators on the Internet that can help you figure this out.*

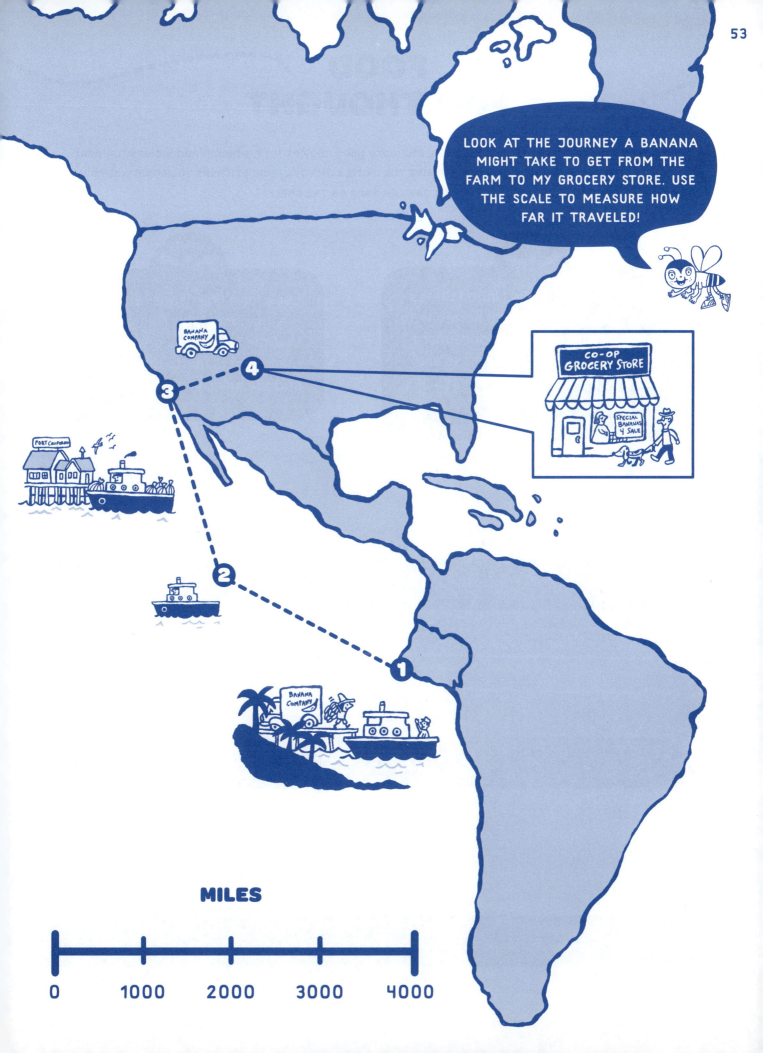

FOOD FOR THOUGHT

When he goes shopping, Buzzle Bee wants to make good choices for his health and the environment. **LOOK AT THE HINTS BELOW, AND THEN EXAMINE THE LABELS ON YOUR FOOD STICKERS TO DECIDE WHERE THEY BELONG—IN BUZZLE BEE'S SHOPPING CART OR BACK ON THE SHELF!**

HINT

Some farmers in the United States give an artificial growth hormone to cows to make them produce more milk. It is unhealthy for cows and may be linked with some types of cancer in humans.

HINT

Look for a Fair Trade label when buying chocolate. This means that the cocoa was grown in a place that is fair to the workers and the environment.

HINT

To be labeled "organic," a food has to be produced by farmers who avoid the use of harmful chemicals, pesticides, and fertilizers. Organic farmers emphasize the use of renewable resources and the conservation of soil and water. Fruits and vegetables that are not organic are sometimes labeled "conventional" in grocery stores.

HINT

Larger fish that live longer have higher amounts of mercury in them than smaller fish. Mercury is poisonous to humans when consumed in large quantities.

FARMERS' MARKETS

Fruits and vegetables that are shipped from distant states and countries can spend as many as 7 to 14 days in transit before they arrive in the supermarket. You can get fresher food and support your local community if you choose foods that are grown in nearby farms or community gardens. **USING THE HARVEST CALENDAR BELOW, DECIDE WHAT BUZZLE BEE SHOULD EAT IN EACH SITUATION DESCRIBED ON THE RIGHT.**

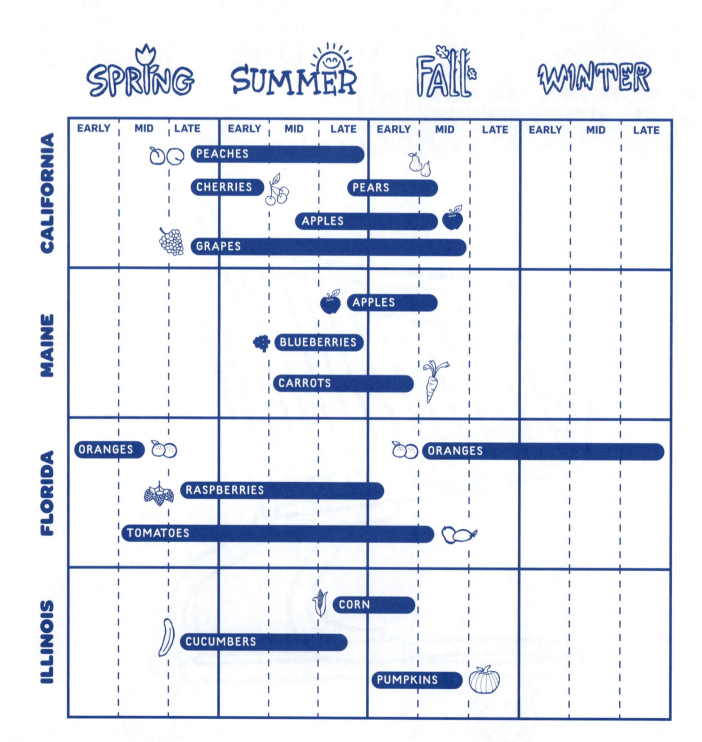

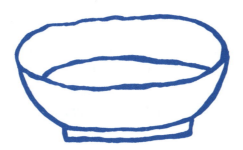

I'M IN CALIFORNIA IN THE EARLY SUMMER. WHAT SHOULD I HAVE IN MY FRUIT SALAD? PUT A STICKER FOR EACH FRUIT IN MY BOWL.

I'M IN MAINE IN THE MIDDLE OF THE SUMMER. WHAT KIND OF PIE SHOULD I HAVE? PUT A FRUIT STICKER ON MY PIE TO SHOW THE BEST CHOICE.

I'M IN FLORIDA FOR THE WINTER. SHOULD I HAVE ORANGES OR RASPBERRIES FOR A SNACK? PUT A STICKER IN MY HAND TO SHOW WHAT'S IN SEASON.

I'M IN ILLINOIS IN THE LATE SUMMER. WHICH VEGETABLES SHOULD I EAT WITH MY DINNER? PUT A STICKER ON MY PLATE FOR EACH VEGETABLE IN SEASON.

TAKE A BREATH

Asthma is a lung disease. If you happen to have asthma, you know that during an asthma attack, the tubes that carry air into your lungs get narrow, making it difficult to breathe. Triggers are pollutants in the environment that can cause people with asthma to have an attack. What choices can you make to help reduce asthma triggers in your home, neighborhood, and on Earth? **SEE IF YOU CAN FIND ALL THE POSSIBLE ASTHMA TRIGGERS IN THIS ENVIRONMENT. PLACE A SNEEZE STICKER ON EACH TRIGGER.**

WASH 'EM WELL!

Many farmers use chemical pesticides, which are potentially toxic to people and animals, to keep crops healthy. Some kinds of produce, like the ones listed below, are grown in environments that have more pesticides than others. When you are buying these kinds of produce, choose organic whenever possible! Also, make sure you rinse all of your produce to get rid of unwanted pesticides. Just don't do it under a running tap—try to conserve water! **FIND THE FRUITS AND VEGETABLES LISTED BELOW IN THE WORD SEARCH.**

```
E P T E I X Z P B A P P L E S G
I L W S R E P P E P L L E B B X
G W A M V R E B L C C K S G Z C
V Q A K Y D N T H R C Z U K X T
B S T R A W B E R R I E S U W Y
G X V L B N R Y R E L E C Q C A
R Z Y J E R S Y E S T O R R A C
E R E L I T S E T V K Y B N Q K
A K G E B O T P P D G R I H A M
E A S U A E B U T A Q S R A E P
P E A C H E S X C R R O V W H S
W G O Q F H N K B E Z G X G D E
```

- CELERY
- KALE
- PEARS
- LETTUCE
- CHERRIES
- APPLES
- GRAPES
- CARROTS
- PEACHES
- BELL PEPPERS
- STRAWBERRIES

HINT: *Some are written backward.*

THINK GLOBALLY

Read these descriptions about some places around the world where human health is affected by the health of the environment. If people everywhere work to make Earth a healthier place, we can all be healthier, too! **USE THE KEY BELOW TO DECODE A PLACE WHERE AND A DATE WHEN EACH PROBLEM HAPPENED.**

JELLY JITTERS

Jellyfish populations bloom and drift closer to shore, posing a greater risk of stinging to swimmers. Researchers think overfishing of the jellyfish's natural predators is partly responsible.

FEISTY FLOODS

More frequent storms with extreme amounts of rain occur, wreaking havoc and uprooting people from their homes.

MOSQUITO MOVEMENT

As temperatures rise, higher elevations become more hospitable to mosquitoes. They are spreading to areas where they have not been found before. Mosquitoes can carry dangerous diseases.

SIMPLE STEPS

LOOK FOR LOCAL FOODS
The next time you go shopping with your family, pay attention to the stickers on foods such as fruits and vegetables. Find out where the foods were grown. See how many foods you can find that come from your local area and give them a try!

GROW YOUR OWN
Have you ever grown your own fruits or vegetables? Even with just a window box, you can grow some pretty tasty fresh herbs. Get some friends or classmates and decide if there is a place to start a community garden in a park, backyard, or your school yard.

THINK BEFORE EATING
Always read the labels on foods and think about what you are about to eat.
USE THE CHART BELOW AND KEEP TRACK OF ALL THE FOOD YOU EAT IN ONE DAY.

BREAKFAST	LUNCH	SNACKS	DINNER

Did you make the best health decisions for yourself?
Did you make the best health decisions for our environment?
Did you read the labels?
Were the foods free of chemicals?
Was the food grown locally?

WASTE & RECYCLING

WASTE

Waste comes in many forms. It's the junk we don't need. It's food scraps. It's paper, grass, and leaves. It's plastic, glass, and metal. It is everything that is thrown out. No matter how you describe waste, one thing is for sure. There is a lot of it!

We "throw away" trash all the time. We toss it in a can. We put it by the curb. We take it to a dump. But we can never really make trash disappear. It just goes to a new place.

RECYCLING

The good news is that much of our trash can be recycled. "Recycling" means to use something again. Recycling often saves energy. For instance, manufacturing recycled paper uses only half as much energy and a tenth as much water as creating paper from new materials. It also saves natural resources through conservation. When you recycle something that has already been made, it means you don't have to make a new one out of valuable natural materials. It is also important to practice the other two Rs: reducing and reusing. You can have fun and help Earth by always being on the lookout for ways to prevent materials from ending up in the garbage.

WHAT AM I?

There are lots of different kinds of materials that you can recycle. Can you think of even more examples of things you can recycle? **PLACE A MATCHING STICKER ABOVE THE LABEL FOR EACH MATERIAL. THEN WRITE AN EXAMPLE OF SOMETHING THAT YOU CAN RECYCLE AT HOME THAT IS MADE FROM THIS SAME MATERIAL.**

ALUMINUM

CARDBOARD

GLASS

MIXED PAPER

PLASTIC

YARD WASTE

TALKING TRASH

Every year, the trash made by people is enough to fill a line of garbage trucks that would stretch from Earth, halfway to the moon. How much trash do you think you make? What natural resources do you think you could save? Do the math to find out.

TAKING OUT THE TRASH

People in the United States are making more waste each year. In 1960, the United States produced about 88 million tons of trash each day. That is about 2.7 pounds per person. Today, people in the United States make over 230 million tons of trash each day. That is roughly 4.5 pounds per person each day! How much trash does that mean each person makes in one year? **COLOR THE TRASH CANS TO SHOW ROUGHLY HOW MUCH TRASH ONE PERSON PRODUCES IN A YEAR. EACH TRASH CAN REPRESENTS 50 POUNDS.**

TREE TROUBLES

How many trees do you think are cut down just to make Sunday newspapers across the country each week? **PLACE THE CORRESPONDING NUMBER OF TREE STICKERS IN THE BOX BELOW. EACH TREE STICKER REPRESENTS 100,000 TREES.**

For one week, collect all the paper and paper products that you would have thrown out. Then weigh it. Ask your teacher to try this with your class.

How much did it all weigh? _____ POUNDS

PAPER OR PLASTIC

Americans use 2,500,000 plastic bottles every hour! Most of them are discarded. How many bottles is that in a 12-hour period? _____ BOTTLES

COLOR THE PLASTIC BOTTLES TO SHOW HOW MUCH AMERICANS USE IN A 12-HOUR PERIOD. EACH BOTTLE IN THE DRAWING REPRESENTS 1,000,000 BOTTLES.

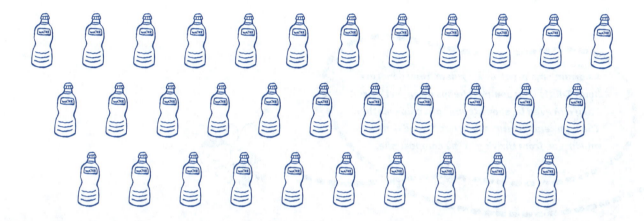

CAN IT!

Recycling just one single aluminum can save enough energy to power a TV for 3 hours. Making a can from scratch uses much more energy because the raw materials have to be mined using big machines. Then the materials have to be transported to a plant and broken down. Recycled cans skip much of this process. **KEEP TRACK OF HOW MANY CANS YOUR FAMILY RECYCLES IN A WEEK. THEN COLOR IN THE TV SETS TO SHOW HOW MANY HOURS OF ENERGY YOU SAVED. EACH TV REPRESENTS 3 HOURS.**

THROW AWAY THE RIGHT WAY

When it's time to throw something away, it's important to think about the most Earth-friendly way to do it. Does it go in a trash can, a recycle bin, or a compost pile? Or is it so hazardous to the environment that it requires a special kind of disposal? You can read about compost piles and hazardous waste disposal on the right. Then decide how best to throw away the twelve waste stickers you'll find on the sticker pages. **DECIDE WHICH THREE WASTE STICKERS BELONG IN EACH BIN.**

As organisms break down waste, they generate heat. This is why compost heaps often feel warm. They can even be seen steaming in cold weather. The high temperatures help keep weeds, insects, and larvae from thriving in the compost pile.

COMPOST

Compost forms as a result of the natural breakdown of organic material. Bacteria, fungi, insects, and animals all break it down to a soil-like material. Once it is made, compost can be used to fertilize soil. It can also be used as mulch in order to reduce the growth of weeds. To make compost, put all your kitchen waste and garden waste in a bin. Do not include anything that cannot break down organically, or any meat, fish, or dairy products.

HAZARDOUS WASTE

Some kinds of waste, such as chemicals and electrical equipment, should never be thrown in the trash. These materials may be dangerous for the environment and need a special kind of disposal, like a special hazardous waste collection center in your area. They need to be kept out of landfills.

TOO FULL

Landfills are not just dumps. They are made to keep trash contained. Each landfill has a huge, chemical-resistant liner that keeps trash in. Many of our landfills desperately need repair so they won't leak. If they do, trash can leak into our water and poison both the water and the land. A large amount of solid waste is disposed of in landfills. So much of the trash that ends up in a landfill doesn't belong there. Look carefully at this heap of garbage. What could have been recycled? What could have been composted? What is hazardous waste that should not be here?

DRAW AN "X" THROUGH EVERYTHING THAT DOESN'T BELONG.

HOW DOES IT WORK?

Aluminum cans are 100 percent recyclable. They can appear on the grocery store shelf just 60 days after being placed in a recycling bin! Look at the pictures that show what happens in the life of an aluminum can. **CAN YOU PUT THE PATH IN ORDER? START WITH THE CAN ON THE STORE SHELF AND DRAW A LINE FROM STEP TO STEP.**

CANS ARE SOLD AT A STORE.

USED CANS ARE COLLECTED IN A RECYCLE BIN.

CANS ARE SHREDDED.

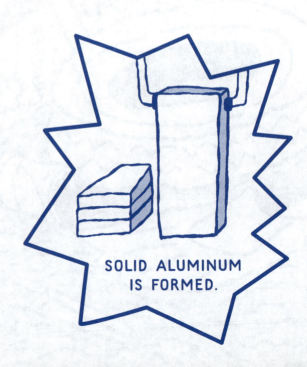

SOLID ALUMINUM IS FORMED.

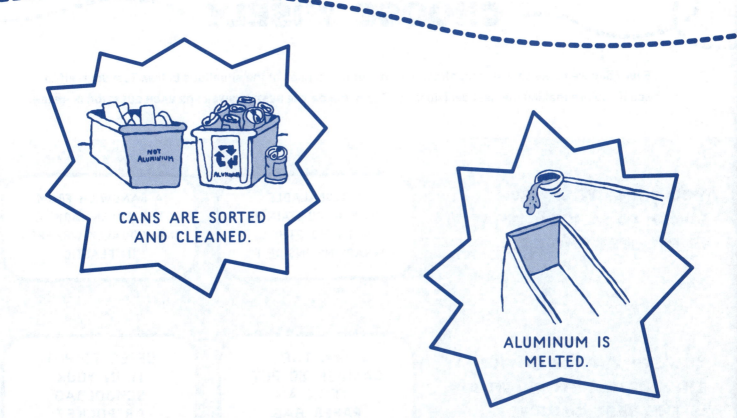

CHOOSE WISELY

Every day we make choices that affect our environment. Look at the situations below. Test yourself to see if you are making the best decisions for Earth. **COLOR THE BEST ANSWER FOR EACH QUESTION IN GREEN.**

YOU BRING YOUR OWN LUNCH TO SCHOOL. WHAT IS THE BEST CHOICE?

- A RESEALABLE PLASTIC CONTAINER WITH NO OTHER WRAPPING INSIDE IT
- A SANDWICH FROM THE SUPERMARKET, INDIVIDUALLY WRAPPED IN PLASTIC

YOU BUY A PACK OF GUM AT THE CORNER STORE. WHAT IS THE BEST CHOICE?

- ASK THE CASHIER TO PUT IT IN A PAPER BAG
- OFFER TO PUT IT IN YOUR SCHOOLBAG OR POCKET

YOU TAKE WATER TO YOUR SPORTS PRACTICE. WHAT IS THE BEST CHOICE?

- TAKE A REUSABLE BOTTLE
- BUY A PLASTIC BOTTLE AND RECYCLE IT

YOU HAVE TO DO RESEARCH USING THE INTERNET FOR A REPORT. WHAT IS THE BEST CHOICE?

- FIND LOTS OF PAGES OF INFORMATION AND PRINT THEM ALL OUT
- BOOKMARK THE PAGES IN YOUR FAVORITES OR DOWNLOAD THEM TO YOUR DESKTOP SO THAT YOU CAN LOOK AT THEM OFF-LINE

Packaging makes up about one-third of our trash. It's not all fast-food boxes, plastic bags, and soda cans. A lot of it is made up of layers of plastic stretch wrap and wooden crates. These are things that keep goods safe before they reach stores. What kinds of packaging can you recycle or reuse?

TWICE IS NICE

LOOK AT THESE COMMON HOUSEHOLD OBJECTS. THINK OF ONE OR MORE WAYS YOU COULD REUSE EACH ITEM AND DRAW AND LABEL YOUR IDEAS. GET CREATIVE!

 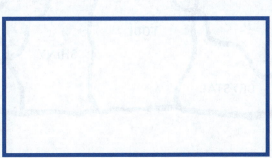

73

THINK GLOBALLY

Some countries produce a lot more trash than others. In fact, the number-one waste producer creates 40 percent of the world's trash all by itself! **TO FIND OUT THE TWO BIGGEST WASTE-PRODUCING COUNTRIES, COLOR IN THE SHAPES THAT CONTAIN THE WORD "WASTE" OR A SYNONYM FOR "WASTE." THEN SEE IF YOU CAN IDENTIFY THE TWO COUNTRIES BY THEIR SHAPES!**

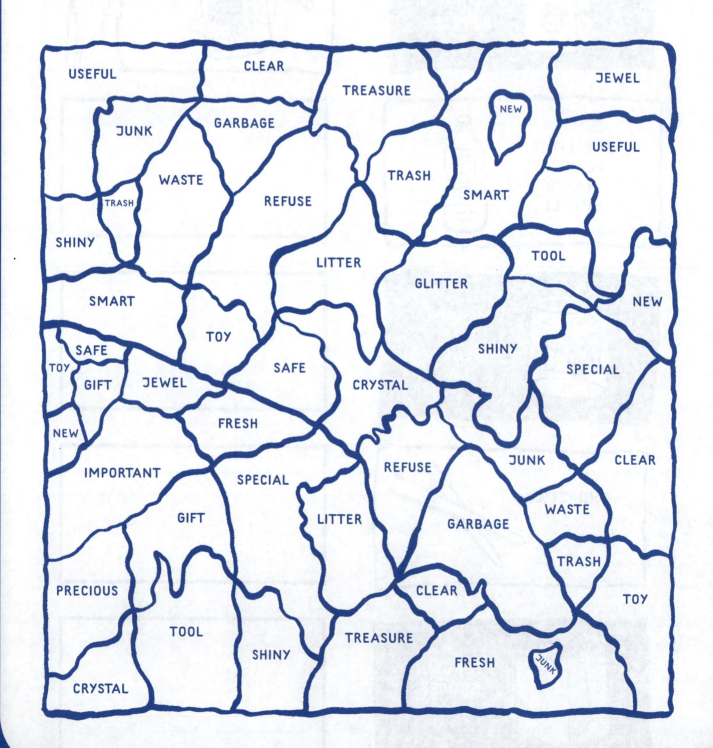

SIMPLE STEPS

JUST SAY NO
Don't let grocery stores put your items in plastic or paper bags. Take a reusable bag with you. And don't forget to take your old plastic and paper bags back to the grocery store for reuse or recycling. Many grocery stores have convenient paper and plastic recycling bins located near the entrance.

DOUBLE UP
Set aside a box for paper that has only been used on one side. Use that paper for notes, or feed the blank side into your printer for draft documents. You can also make scratch pads out of that single-sided paper by binding it.

GO PAPERLESS
Can you go paperless? Ask your teacher if you can hand in assignments via e-mail instead of on paper.

BE A SMART SHOPPER
Make sure to pick products that have been made using recycled materials. Especially look for this in paper products, such as toilet paper and paper towels. In fact, try to avoid paper towels when possible. Encourage your family to use reusable cloth products for cleaning.

ANSWERS
ENERGY AND CLIMATE

P. 7
Gasoline Oil
Electricity Propane

41% Heating / 26% Lighting and appliances / 20% Water heater / 8% Air conditioning / 5% Refrigeration

P. 8-9
PLACES WHERE ENERGY IS BEING WASTED:

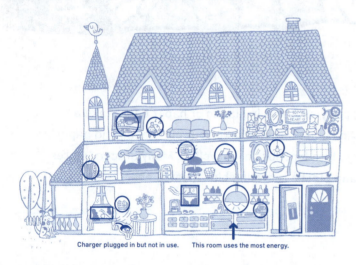
Charger plugged in but not in use. This room uses the most energy.

P. 10
Refrigerator: 1 / Dryer: 2 / Microwave: 3 / Television: 4 / Table lamp: 5

P. 11
NEED FUEL TO WORK: Airplane / Truck / Train / Bus / Motor scooter / Motorboat

BIGGEST ENERGY USER: Airplane

P. 14
RENEWABLE: Wind / Sun (solar energy) / Water (hydro-power) / Corn oil (biomass fuel)

NON-RENEWABLE: Gas (stove and car) / Oil / Propane (grill)

P. 15
DOWN: 1. Hydropower / 2. Methane / 3. Oil / 4. Fossil (Fuels) / 6. Uranium

ACROSS: 5. Coal / 7. Ethanol / 8. Electricity / 9. Biomass

P. 16
POSITIVE STEPS: Take the stairs / Use sunlight instead of a lamp / Plant a tree / Unplug all electrical chargers when not in use / Carpool / Ride a bike to school / Put on a sweater instead of turning up the heat / Dry your clothes in the sun

P. 18
ARROWS FROM LEFT TO RIGHT: Yellow, Red, Green

P. 19
Meteorology / Drought / Tornado / Precipitation / Flood / Hurricane / El Niño

A HURRICANE IN THE WESTERN PACIFIC OCEAN IS CALLED A: Typhoon

P. 20
1. United States
2. China
3. Russia
4. Japan
5. India
6. Germany
7. United Kingdom
8. Canada
9. Italy
10. Mexico

ANSWERS
WATER AND OCEANS

P. 23

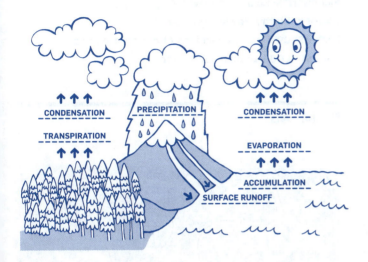

P. 26–27
EARTH-FRIENDLY PRODUCTS: Vinegar / Phosphate-free detergent / Lemon juice / Compost
POISON: Bleach / Chemical fertilizer / Chemical pesticide / Motor oil

P. 28–29
THREATENED
Wild Atlantic salmon - *This popular fish has been overfished nearly to the point of extinction. Parts of its habitat are now protected under the Endangered Species Act.*

Black sea bass - *The demand for this popular fish is greater than the supply. It has been greatly overfished in the South Atlantic.*

Nassau grouper - *This fish was once one of the most important commercial fish of the Caribbean. It is now protected from fishing and is on the International Union for Conservation of Nature's Red List of endangered species.*

Yellow tail flounder - *The population levels of this sandy-bottom fish are now very low. The trawls used to catch it can also damage the ocean floor and disrupt the flounder's habitat.*

SUSTAINABLE
Pacific halibut / Striped bass / Tilapia / Alaska wild salmon

P. 30
PLASTIC IN THE OCEAN:

P. 31
TOP ROW: Gray whale / Blue whale / Humpback whale
BOTTOM ROW: Narwhal / Bowhead whale / Right whale

P. 32
The white area shows the size of the remaining portion of the summer ice cap. The shape is not exact. This is just to show the approximate change in size.

P. 33
FROM TOP TO BOTTOM: Orca / Seal / Penguin / Fish / Krill / Plankton

P. 34
Ethiopia / Afghanistan

ANSWERS
LAND AND ANIMALS

P. 37
EXTINCT: Passenger pigeon / Caribbean monk seal
ENDANGERED: Mountain gorilla / Giant panda
VULNERABLE: Cheetah / African lion

P. 38–39
THINGS THAT MIGHT BE POLLUTING THE ENVIRONMENT:

P. 40
EVERGLADES: Alligator / Pelican
TUNDRA: Walrus / Arctic fox
SAVANNA: Giraffe / Zebra

P. 41

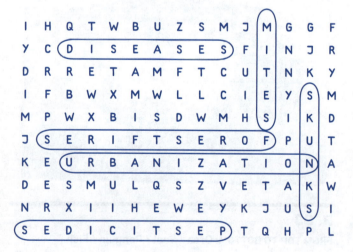

P. 42–43
EMERGENTS: Scarlet macaw / Harpy eagle
CANOPY: Sloth / Howler monkey
UNDERSTORY: Poison dart frog / Emerald tree boa
FOREST FLOOR: Jaguar / Anteater

P. 44–45

P. 46
TRUE: Wolves are the ancestors of all breeds of domestic dogs. Wolves are the largest members of the canine family. Wolves once lived in all of the lower 48 states.

FALSE: Wolves kill as many as 10 people each year. All gray wolf populations are stable and do not need protection. Wolves may soon wipe out elk populations.

P. 47
DIFFERENCES BETWEEN GRIZZLY BEAR AND BLACK BEAR:

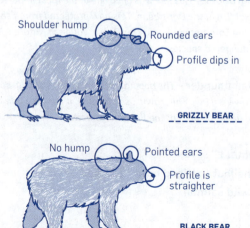

ANSWERS
HEALTH AND FOOD

P. 48
FROM INSIDE TO OUTSIDE: Brazil / Zambia / Myanmar / Indonesia / Nigeria

P. 51
ORANGES: Brazil
CANTALOUPE: Guatemala
GRAPES: Chile
STRAWBERRIES: Mexico
PEARS: Argentina
KIWI: New Zealand

P. 52–53
Buzzle Bee's banana traveled about 5,000 miles.

P. 54–55
THINGS THAT BELONG IN BUZZLE BEE'S CART:
Fair trade chocolate bar / Sardines / Organic vegetables / Local milk / Organic chicken

P. 56–57
CALIFORNIA: Peaches / Cherries / Grapes
MAINE: Blueberries
FLORIDA: Oranges
ILLINOIS: Corn / Cucumber

P. 58

P. 59

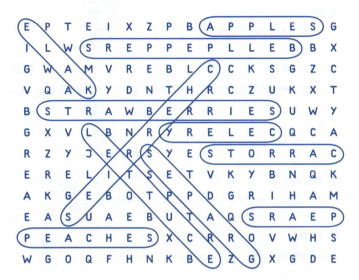

P. 60
JELLY JITTERS: Barcelona, Spain, 2007
FIESTY FLOODS: Midwest, USA, 2008
MOSQUITO MOVEMENT: Nairobi, Kenya, 2008

79

ANSWERS
WASTE AND RECYCLING

P. 63
ALUMINUM:
Possible answers: *tuna can, soup can*

CARDBOARD:
Possible answers: *back of a notepad, packing materials*

GLASS:
Possible answers: *jelly jar, baby food jar*

MIXED PAPER:
Possible answers: *magazines, office paper*

PLASTIC:
Possible answers: *grocery bags, milk container*

YARD WASTE:
Possible answers: *grass clippings, twigs*

P. 64–65
The average person produces about **1,642.5 pounds** each year. **(ALMOST 33 TRASH CANS)**

500,000 trees are cut down each week, just to make Sunday newspapers. **(5 TREE STICKERS)**

Americans use **30,000,000** plastic bottles in a 12-hour period. **(30 BOTTLES)**

P. 66–67
COMPOST: Coffee grounds / Apple peel / Leaves

TRASH: Chicken leg / Fish / Diaper

HAZARDOUS WASTE: Batteries / Antifreeze / Old computer

RECYCLING BIN: Shredded newspaper / Plastic bottle / Aluminum can

P. 68–69
THESE THINGS DO NOT BELONG IN THE LANDFILL:

P. 70–71
Cans are sold at a store. ➔ Used cans are collected in a recycle bin. ➔ Cans are sorted and cleaned. ➔ Cans are shredded. ➔ Aluminum is melted. ➔ Solid aluminum is formed. ➔ Cans are manufactured.

P. 72
BEST CHOICES: A resealable plastic container with no other wrapping inside it / Offer to put it in your schoolbag or pocket / Take a reusable bottle / Bookmark the pages in your favorites or download them to your desktop so that you can look at them off-line

P. 74
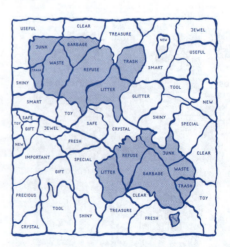

The **United States** and **Australia** are the two biggest waste-producing countries.

31

RIGHT

BOWHEAD

GRAY

HUMPBACK

NARWHAL

BLUE

9

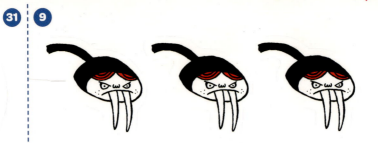

33

FISH

PLANKTON

PENGUIN

SEAL

ORCA

KRILL

40

ARCTIC FOX · WALRUS · GIRAFFE · PELICAN · ZEBRA · ALLIGATOR

54

CONVENTIONAL ORGANIC

SARDINES TUNA

ORGANIC EASY MILK

FACTORY FARM LOCAL MILK NO HORMONES

Yummy Chocolate

FAIR TRADE CHOCOLATE BAR

37
- CHEETAH
- GIANT PANDA
- PASSENGER PIGEON
- MOUNTAIN GORILLA
- CARIBBEAN MONK SEAL
- AFRICAN LION

42
- SLOTH
- JAGUAR
- POISON DART FROG
- HOWLER MONKEY
- EMERALD TREE BOA
- SCARLET MACAW
- HARPY EAGLE
- ANTEATER

57

58 ACHOO! ACHOO! ACHOO! ACHOO! ACHOO! ACHOO! ACHOO!

63

64

66
- COFFEE GROUNDS
- BATTERIES
- DIAPER
- CHICKEN LEG
- ANTIFREEZE
- PLASTIC BOTTLE
- ALUMINUM CAN
- OLD COMPUTER
- FISH
- APPLE PEEL
- SHREDDED NEWSPAPER
- LEAVES